Table of Contents

Introduction

Hello Reader! I am glad that you decided to broaden your knowledge of Entity Framework Core 5. I can assure you that I have spent several months thoroughly researching EF Core documentation and testing its possibilities in practice. I wrote a few projects in Entity Framework and EF Core, so in this book I decided to focus on practice and my own experience with this technology. For me, when working with EF Core, the most important thing was its simplicity and minimalism. With relatively little effort, you can work with EF Core extremely efficiently, using its best capabilities.

In this book, you will find extensive code snippets that use EF Core. They are part of a larger project called PrimeHotel which is available on my Github account. I strongly encourage you to try your hand at Entity Framework Core 5 yourself, and the PrimeHotel project can be a very good starting point.

About the author

My name is Michał Białecki. I am a .Net / C # developer with over 10 years of experience. I am passionate about exploring the possibilities of the Azure cloud and news in the .NET world. For over 3 years I have been running a blog http://michalbialecki.com, which has several thousand users every month.

I've been learning and using Entity Framework for quite a few years, and I just fell in love with Entity Framework Core - it's amazing! I am sure that my passion will infect you too!

Feel free to contact me via social media. Find me on:

 https://www.linkedin.com/in/michal-bialecki/

 https://github.com/mikuam/PrimeHotel

 Michał Białecki Blog

 https://www.instagram.com/mik.bialecki/

Demonstration project

The PrimeHotel project can be found here:
https://github.com/mikuam/PrimeHotel.

PrimeHotel is developed in ASP.NET Core technology in .NET 5, and Entity Framework Core 5. It is an API for simple operations in the hotel system, such as adding a guest or creating a reservation. With this example, I will discuss in detail the capabilities of EF Core and demonstrate how to use it.

Below you will find a step-by-step instruction on how to run it.

First, make sure you have Git installed on your computer. Then you can clone the project with the command in Terminal.

```
git clone https://github.com/mikuam/PrimeHotel.git
```

Now, open the project in your favourite IDE such as Visual Studio or Visual Studio Code. I'm using Visual Studio 2019 and it looks like this on my computer.

- Solution 'PrimeHotel' (2 of 2 projects)
  - PrimeHotel.Web
    - Connected Services
    - Dependencies
    - Properties
    - Clients
      - IWeatherStackClient.cs
      - WeatherStackClient.cs
      - WeatherStackResponse.cs
    - Controllers
      - LiveWeatherForecastController.cs
      - NewReservation.cs
      - ProfileController.cs
      - ProfileWithDapperController.cs
      - ReservationsController.cs
      - RoomController.cs
      - WeatherForecast.cs
      - WeatherForecastController.cs
      - WeatherForecastFilters.cs
    - Data
      - IProfilesRepository.cs
      - ProfilesRepository.cs
    - Migrations
    - Models
      - Address.cs
      - GuestArrival.cs
      - PrimeDbContext.cs
      - Profile.cs
      - Reservation.cs
      - Room.cs
      - RoomOccupied.cs
    - appsettings.json
    - Program.cs
    - Startup.cs
  - PrimeHotel.Web.Tests

Now let's take a look at the structure of the project:

- ▶ Clients - here are classes that communicate with other services using HttpClient
- ▶ Controllers - Here are all controller classes containing all endpoints in this service
- ▶ Data - repository classes that contain SQL commands - currently Dapper
- ▶ Migrations - Entity Framework Core 5 migrations that persist database schema changes
- ▶ Models - Entity Framework Core 5 classes that mirror the tables in the database

Database configuration

For educational purposes, the easiest option is to set up SQL Server on your computer. However, if you want to set it as a docker image, you can read how to do it in my post here: https://www.michalbialecki.com/2020/04/23/set-up-a-sql-server-in-a-docker -container

You can download the SQL Server Express version for free from the Microsoft website: https://www.microsoft.com/pl-pl/sql-server/sql-server-downloads. After the server is installed and configured, it will likely be available with localhost. Try to connect to SQL Server and check that your connection is working correctly. Then create a blank database called PrimeHotel. I use Azure Data Studio to connect to the database - a clear and fast tool, perfect for simple tasks.

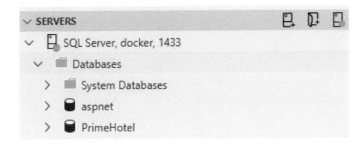

The last step is to change the connection string in the project. To do this, edit the appsettings.json file. It looks like this:

```
{
  "ConnectionStrings": {
    "HotelDB": "Data Source=localhost;Initial Catalog=PrimeHotel;Integrated
Security=True"
  },
  "Logging": {
    "LogLevel": {
      "Default": "Information",
      "Microsoft": "Warning",
      "Microsoft.Hosting.Lifetime": "Information"
    }
  },
  "AllowedHosts": "*"
}
```

The connection string may be slightly different, but mine looks just like the one above.

Instead of the *localhost*, you can have something similar to *localhost\SQLEXPRESS*, but the exact address depends on the SQL Server configuration.

Project launch

When everything is ready, you can start the project. Remember that you also need to have .NET 5 runtime and SDK installed.

In Visual Studio, you can just press F5. In Visual Studio Code, open a terminal window and enter the two commands: *dotnet build* and *dotnet run*. Then, go to the link in your browser that will be displayed on the console. You should see something like this:

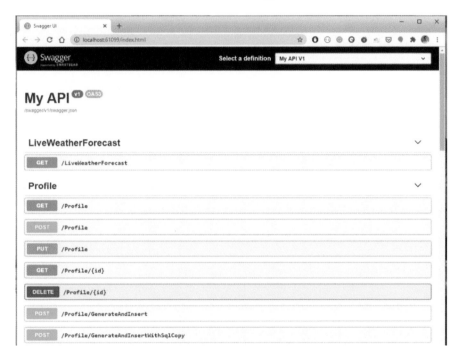

Simple, isn't it? Congratulations, you have just launched PrimeHotel. Now you can start coding, modifying, testing and improving this service. Let's do this!

Ideas for your own project

You might already have some ideas for what to write and build on your own. However, if you're not sure of what might be a good candidate, here are some ideas. To fully utilize the possibilities of Entity Framework Core, you need to think of a project from the database perspective. The best idea would have such a database structure, so you can try out relationships of a different kind.

Here are some ideas you might find inspiring:

- ► Book library
- ► Reddit
- ► Highway toll
- ► Movie catalogue, like IMDb
- ► Loyalty club
- ► Grades online
- ► Flight tickets system

Actually, there are no bad ideas. The most important thing is to choose something that you'd like to create. Start small and take multiple small steps. Don't aim to build production ready app just yet, it doesn't have to be perfect from the start.

Entity Framework, the new way

Entity Framework Core 5 is a lightweight, efficient, open source technology for working with a database. EF Core is an object-relational (O/RM) mapper that makes working with a database simple and fun. Instead of writing SQL queries, you can just use objects and methods in your C# code.

The predecessor of Entity Framework Core is Entity Framework, which debuted in 2008 and presented a modern approach of working with the database. It allows you to work with data in the form of domain objects, without going into details of how the data is represented in the database. Entity Framework also has a graphical editor that allows you to generate model classes from the database without writing any code or commands. It is also possible to define the model on the code side and generate a migration to update the database. EF has been developed over many years and is stable and tested. However, it is not void of mistakes. The model and its mapping in the database in Entity Framework is saved in the EDMX file, but working with it is not as convenient as it could be. With larger databases, the graphics editor slowed down severely, forcing the developer to manually edit this file.

Entity Framework Core has been rewritten and no longer relies on EDMX file. The configuration itself has been kept to a minimum, and in most cases the mapping will be done automatically, following the convention. Certainly EF Core is also faster than its predecessor, but there is no significant difference in terms of the offered possibilities. A comparison of these two frameworks is available here: https://docs.microsoft.com/pl-pl/ef/efcore-and-ef6/.

An important declaration by Microsoft is that Entity Framework 6 will be its last version and will no longer be actively developed. Hence, all new functionalities will be implemented in Entity Framework Core.

Supported frameworks and operating systems

Both Entity Framework 6 and Entity Framework Core support .NET Core, which means they can be developed and run on Windows, MacOs, and Linux.

Entity Framework Core 5 supports .NET Standard from version 2.1, which means it can run on multiple platforms and technologies, such as .NET Core from version 3.0 and .NET 5, Xamarin and Mono.

Warning! EF Core 5 does not support the .NET Framework and therefore cannot be used in older projects.

So… should I use Entity Framework Core 5?

If you are starting a new project, the answer is certainly yes. If you plan to significantly expand an existing project, this will also be a good choice. However, if you already have a large stable project based on Entity Framework, migrating to EF Core may not always pay off. Code working with EF will not be fully compatible with EF Core, and better performance depends on how you use the database. So, it is best if you check it first in the form of Proof Of Concept to see whether or not it is really profitable.

Getting started with EF Core

You don't need to sweat much to add Entity Framework Core 5 to your project. In this chapter, I will explain how to add EF Core to an ASP.NET Core application and to a console application.

In an API application in ASP.NET Core

If you're building a new app to learn about EF Core's capabilities, it's best to generate it with .NET CLI. Just open a console window and type the command:

```
dotnet new webapi --name ApiTest
```

This command will create a project named ApiTest. It will be an ASP.NET Core project with one sample controller, which is enough to get you started. The only thing I would add is Swagger, which is an interactive API documentation. It can query our API and display the results transparently and graphically.

You can find out how to install Swagger in ASP.NET Core here: https://docs.microsoft.com/pl-pl/aspnet/core/tutorials/getting-started-with-swashbuckle

The Entity Framework Core installation starts with the installation of 2 NuGet packages:
- ▶ Microsoft.EntityFrameworkCore
- ▶ Microsoft.EntityFrameworkCore.SqlServer

At this point, we can use the Database First approach and map an existing table from the database. To add a table with cars, execute the following SQL command, e.g. in Azure Data Studio:

```
CREATE TABLE [dbo].[Cars](
    [Id] [int] IDENTITY(1,1) NOT NULL,
    [RegistrationNumber] [nvarchar](max) NOT NULL,
    [Make] [nvarchar](max) NULL,
    [Model] [nvarchar](max) NULL,
    [CompanyCar] [bit] NOT NULL,
 CONSTRAINT [PK_Cars] PRIMARY KEY CLUSTERED
(
    [Id] ASC
)WITH (PAD_INDEX = OFF, STATISTICS_NORECOMPUTE = OFF, IGNORE_DUP_KEY = OFF,
 ALLOW_ROW_LOCKS = ON, ALLOW_PAGE_LOCKS = ON) ON [PRIMARY]
) ON [PRIMARY] TEXTIMAGE_ON [PRIMARY]
GO
```

To add a car model in the project, create the *Models* folder and add a class inside with the *DbContext* ending, which will look like this:

```
public class PrimeDbContext : DbContext
{
    public PrimeDbContext(DbContextOptions<PrimeDbContext> options)
        : base(options)
    {
    }

    public virtual DbSet<Car> Cars { get; set; }
}
```

We also add the *Car* entity to represent the row in the *Cars* table.

```
public class Car
{
    public int Id { get; set; }

    public string RegistrationNumber { get; set; }

    public string Make { get; set; }

    public string Model { get; set; }

    public bool CompanyCar { get; set; }
}
```

We already have the *PrimeDbContext* class, now it's time to configure it. In ASP.NET Core, the configuration is stored in the appsettings.json file, so add the *ConnectionStrings* section there and add our connection to the database.

```
{
  "ConnectionStrings": {
    "HotelDB": "Data Source=localhost;Initial Catalog=PrimeHotel;Integrated
Security=True"
  },
  "Logging": {
    "LogLevel": {
      "Default": "Information",
      "Microsoft": "Warning",
      "Microsoft.Hosting.Lifetime": "Information"
    }
  },
  "AllowedHosts": "*"
}
```

The connection we will be using is *HotelDB,* and the database is called *PrimeHotel* and it runs on my local server.

The last thing we need to configure is adding a connection to the *PrimeDbContext* initialization in the Dependency Injection container. We need to add the following code to the *ConfigureServices* method in the Startup.cs file:

```
public void ConfigureServices(IServiceCollection services)
{
    // Entity Framework
    services.AddDbContext<PrimeDbContext>(options =>
        options.UseSqlServer(Configuration.GetConnectionString("HotelDB")));
}
```

With EF Core configured in this way, we can start working and use its full potential. To check the results of our work, the easiest way is to use a controller that already exists and add one line in its code:

```
var cars = _dbContext.Cars.ToList();
```

Of course, with the assumption that *PrimeDbContext* class is injected in the controller's constructor and is assigned to a local variable called *_dbContext*. The effect looks like this:

```
[HttpGet]
0 references
public IEnumerable<WeatherForecast> Get()
{
    var cars =  dbContext.Cars.ToList();    cars = Count = 2
                ▲ ● cars     Count = 2 ⊟
    var rng =  ▲ ● [0]           {ApiTest1.Models.Car}
    return Enu ▶  ✦ CompanyCar          false       new WeatherForecast
    {          ▶  ✦ Id                  1
        Date = Da ✦ Make             Q ▾ "Ford"
        Temperatu ✦ Model            Q ▾ "C-Max"
        Summary = ✦ RegistrationNumber  Q ▾ "PO234"  gth)]
    })
    .ToArray();
}
```

In the following chapters, you will learn how to use the Code First approach, i.e. how to update the database based on the class entity created in the code. For this task, we will also need migrations.

In a console application

To build a console application, it is best to execute the command with .NET CLI in the console:

```
dotnet new console --name ConsoleTest
```

This command will create a project named ConsoleTest. It will be a console application with one *Program.cs* file and the *Main* method.

The Entity Framework Core installation starts with the installation of two NuGet packages:
- ▶ Microsoft.EntityFrameworkCore
- ▶ Microsoft.EntityFrameworkCore.SqlServer

At this point, we can use the Database First approach and map an existing table from the database. To add a table with cars, execute the following SQL command, e.g. in Azure Data Studio:

```
CREATE TABLE [dbo].[Cars](
    [Id] [int] IDENTITY(1,1) NOT NULL,
    [RegistrationNumber] [nvarchar](max) NOT NULL,
    [Make] [nvarchar](max) NULL,
    [Model] [nvarchar](max) NULL,
    [CompanyCar] [bit] NOT NULL,
 CONSTRAINT [PK_Cars] PRIMARY KEY CLUSTERED
(
    [Id] ASC
)WITH (PAD_INDEX = OFF, STATISTICS_NORECOMPUTE = OFF, IGNORE_DUP_KEY = OFF,
 ALLOW_ROW_LOCKS = ON, ALLOW_PAGE_LOCKS = ON) ON [PRIMARY]
) ON [PRIMARY] TEXTIMAGE_ON [PRIMARY]
GO
```

To add a car model in a project, create a *Models* folder and add a class inside with the *DbContext* ending, which will look like this:

```
public class PrimeDbContext : DbContext
{
    public PrimeDbContext(DbContextOptions<PrimeDbContext> options)
        : base(options)
    {
    }

    public virtual DbSet<Car> Cars { get; set; }

    protected override void OnConfiguring(DbContextOptionsBuilder op-
tionsBuilder)
    {
        optionsBuilder.UseSqlServer(@"Data Source = localhost; Initial
Catalog = PrimeHotel; Integrated Security = True");
    }
}
```

We also add the *Car* entity, which will represent the row in the *Cars*
table.

```
public class Car
{
    public int Id { get; set; }

    public string RegistrationNumber { get; set; }

    public string Make { get; set; }

    public string Model { get; set; }

    public bool CompanyCar { get; set; }
}
```

We already have the *PrimeDbContext* class, and in the *OnConfiguring*
method we set the connection to our database. As a general rule,
configuration should not be kept in program code. For demonstration
purposes, this approach is fine, but before publishing your code to
GitHub or to the server, it's a good practice to move your
configuration to a separate file.

To test if EF Core is actually working, it is best to modify the program
code like this:

```
class Program
{
    static void Main(string[] args)
    {
        Console.WriteLine("Hello World!");

        using var dbContext = new PrimeDbContext(new
DbContextOptions<PrimeDbContext>());
        var cars = dbContext.Cars.ToList();

    }
}
```

With so little effort, we can already use EF Core. If I stop the program
on the last line, the result will be:

As you can see, adding EF Core to both the API application in ASP.NET
Core and the console application does not require too much work. Its
possibilities are really big. I'll discuss them in more detail in the
following chapters.

Assignments

1. Create your own project of any type and add Entity Framework Core to it. This can be a console application or an ASP.NET Core API. Then follow the steps in this chapter and add a simple table to your database.
   a. Fill in the table with a few rows of data.
   b. Use a class that inherits from *DbContext* in your program code.
   c. Check that the table will be correctly mapped to the collection.
   d. Use *Where* method on the collection to filter it.
2. All EF Core 5 methods have an asynchronous version, ending with *Async*. Please rewrite your application code so that it uses asynchronous methods in EF Core.

Simple CRUD operations

When we have everything in place, the required packages installed, the database set up and the appropriate configuration, we can start using the O/RM mechanism! The simplest operations are CRUD operations which are: Create, Read, Update and Delete. These are the operations that can be performed on the resource, that is: creating a new entry, reading, updating and deleting.

If we translate these operations into HTTP request methods, we get the following pairs:

▶ Create – Post
▶ Read – Get
▶ Update – Put as a replacement for an object or Patch as a partial update
▶ Delete – Delete

It is very simple to implement CRUD operations in an ASP.NET Core controller in .NET 5. All table operations in EF Core must be done with *PrimeDbContext*. When we register it in the Startup.cs class, it will be available in any class to which we can inject it with Dependency Injection. Take a look at this example of simple CRUD operations in *RoomController*.

```csharp
[ApiController]
[Route("[controller]")]
public class RoomController : ControllerBase
{
    private readonly PrimeDbContext primeDbContext;

    public RoomController(PrimeDbContext _primeDbContext)
    {
        primeDbContext = _primeDbContext;
    }

    [HttpGet]
    public async Task<IEnumerable<Room>> Get()
    {
        return await primeDbContext.Rooms.AsNoTracking().ToListAsync();
    }

    [HttpGet("{id}")]
    public async Task<IActionResult> Get(int id)
    {
        var room = await primeDbContext.Rooms.FindAsync(id);
        if (room == null)
        {
            return NotFound();
        }

        return Ok(room);
    }

    [HttpPost]
    public async Task<IActionResult> Post([FromBody] Room room)
    {
        var createdRoom = await primeDbContext.Rooms.AddAsync(room);
        await primeDbContext.SaveChangesAsync();

        return Ok(createdRoom.Entity);
    }

    [HttpPut]
    public async Task<IActionResult> Put([FromBody] Room room)
    {
        var existingRoom = await primeDbContext.Rooms.FindAsync(room.Id);
        if (existingRoom == null)
        {
            return NotFound();
        }

        existingRoom.Number = room.Number;
        existingRoom.Description = room.Description;
        existingRoom.LastBooked = room.LastBooked;
        existingRoom.Level = room.Level;
        existingRoom.RoomType = room.RoomType;
        existingRoom.NumberOfPlacesToSleep = room.NumberOfPlacesToSleep;

        var updatedRoom = primeDbContext.Update(existingRoom);
        await primeDbContext.SaveChangesAsync();
        return Ok(updatedRoom.Entity);
    }
}
```

```
[HttpDelete("{id}")]
public async Task<IActionResult> Delete(int id)
{
    var existingRoom = await primeDbContext.Rooms.FindAsync(id);
    if (existingRoom == null)
    {
        return NotFound();
    }

    var removedRoom = primeDbContext.Rooms.Remove(existingRoom);
    await primeDbContext.SaveChangesAsync();

    return Ok(removedRoom.Entity);
}
```

Note that in EF Core, each method has an asynchronous version. Utilizing asynchronous programming is generally a good idea. This way, your code will be faster and can run more efficiently with many other requests in parallel.

Important things to keep in mind:

▶ We can search entities in a collection with LINQ using the *Where*. We can also use other methods, such as *Select* and *GroupBy*, and they will be translated into a SQL query

▶ If you are only filtering the entities to display, you can use *AsNoTracking()* to improve performance. This returns entities where changes will not be tracked

▶ To be able to make changes to an entity, it must be tracked, i.e. retrieved using the *DbContext* class. That's why in the *Put* method, we first get the entity, change it, and finally save the changes

▶ A database call will only be made when the code we are writing needs results. This happens, for example, when we use the *ToListAsync, First* or *FirstOrDefault* method

▶ All changes we make must be saved with *SaveChanges* or *SaveChangesAsync* to save them in the database

These are just a few points to keep in mind, but there's still a lot more going on below that you should know about. However, this introduction is enough to get you started and is more than enough to get you started with Entity Framework Core on your own.

Assignments

1. Add your own controller and implement CRUD methods
2. Implement a Patch method that will only update the fields in the entity that will be uploaded
   a. Hint: To tell if a field has been passed to the controller, it is best to be represented as a property of type *Nullable<Type>*

Easy work with migrations

Database migrations help the developer keep the database schema with code up-to-date. This is the primary mechanism that updates the database based on code. Migrations in Entity Framework Core 5 are designed to track the *DbContext* class and generate a migration as it updates.

Adding a migration

To manage migrations, the dotnet-ef global tool is best. You can install it by executing the following script:

```
dotnet tool install --global dotnet-ef
```

Then, in the project directory, execute the following command:

```
dotnet ef migrations add InitialCreate
```

The new migration will appear in the Migrations directory.

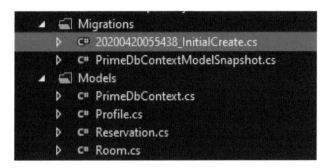

When we add the first migration, the *PrimeDbContextModelSnapshot* file also appears, which represents the current state of the model. It will be updated with subsequent migrations. The migration itself contains the *Up* and *Down* methods, which contain changes to the database when performing and undoing the migration.

Creating a migration makes sense when we make changes to the model. So, let's add a new model class called *Room*.

```
public class Room
{
    public int Id { get; set; }

    public int Number { get; set; }

    public string Description { get; set; }

    public DateTime LastBooked { get; set; }

    public int Level { get; set; }

    public RoomType RoomType { get; set; }

    public int NumberOfPlacesToSleep { get; set; }
}

public enum RoomType
{
    Standard,
    Suite
}
```

And we add the *Rooms* virtual collection to the *PrimeDbContext* class.

```
public class PrimeDbContext : DbContext
{
    public PrimeDbContext(DbContextOptions<PrimeDbContext> options)
        : base(options)
    {
    }

    public virtual DbSet<Room> Rooms { get; set; }

    protected override void OnModelCreating(ModelBuilder modelBuilder)
    {
    }
}
```

In this case, the generated migration will look like this:

```csharp
public partial class InitialCreate : Migration
{
    protected override void Up(MigrationBuilder migrationBuilder)
    {
        migrationBuilder.CreateTable(
            name: "Rooms",
            columns: table => new
            {
                Id = table.Column<int>(nullable: false)
                    .Annotation("SqlServer:Identity", "1, 1"),
                Number = table.Column<int>(nullable: false),
                Description = table.Column<string>(nullable: true),
                LastBooked = table.Column<DateTime>(nullable: false),
                Level = table.Column<int>(nullable: false),
                RoomType = table.Column<int>(nullable: false),
                NumberOfPlacesToSleep = table.Column<int>(nullable: false)
            },
            constraints: table =>
            {
                table.PrimaryKey("PK_Rooms", x => x.Id);
            });
    }

    protected override void Down(MigrationBuilder migrationBuilder)
    {
        migrationBuilder.DropTable(
            name: "Rooms");
    }
}
```

This is what the migration looks like when we add the *Rooms* table. The file will be generated automatically, but will not be automatically updated later when the *Room* model changes. The best thing to do after generating the migration is to have a look at it and see if it does what it should. We can modify the migration according to our needs, so nothing prevents us from introducing our own improvements. Until the migration is performed, you can freely modify it, and even delete it and regenerate it. If it is performed on a database, you shouldn't change it anymore. If you want to make any changes to it, it is best to generate another migration.

We can add next migrations with the command:

```
Dotnet ef migrations add <name>
```

Running the migrations

At this point, you can run Entity Framework Core 5 migrations and update the database schema. You can do this with the following .NET CLI command in a terminal window in your project directory:

```
dotnet ef database update
```

Performed migrations are saved in the database and will not run again. The migration status is stored in the __EFMigrationsHistory

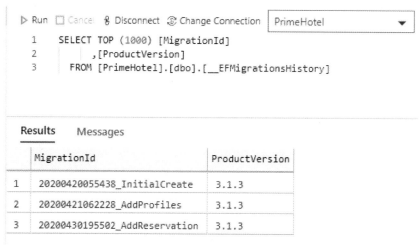

table.

However, there is a way to update the database and perform migrations from application code. It is best to do this at the start of the application, thanks to which we know that the new version of the program will be run on the current database.

To do this, execute the command:

```
context.Database.Migrate();
```

Where *context* is a class that inherits from *DbContext*. This one command will start migrations and update our database.

When building an application in ASP.NET Core, we can add a simple *UpgradeDatabase* method to the Startup.cs file, which will start migrations at the start of our API. Its definition is as follows:

```
private void UpgradeDatabase(IApplicationBuilder app)
{
    using (var serviceScope = app.ApplicationServices.CreateScope())
    {
        var context = serviceScope.ServiceProvider.GetService
                <PrimeDbContext>();
        if (context != null && context.Database != null)
        {
            context.Database.Migrate();
        }
    }
}
```

This method uses the built-in Dependency Injection mechanism to retrieve a *PrimeDbContext* instance and use it to run database migration. Only those migrations that have not yet been performed will run.

Then, in the *Configure* method, add at the end.

```
UpgradeDatabase(app);
```

Thanks to this mechanism, the application will update the database used, regardless of whether it is run locally or it is deployed and run on a production server.

Reverting migrations

With EF Core, you can not only apply pending migrations, but also revert one or more migrations. Thanks to the database update command, we can determine the state of the database. Let's look at an example. Currently, there are a number of migrations in my database and the contents of the __EFMigrationsHistory table are as

	MigrationId	ProductVersion
1	20200420055438_InitialCreate	3.1.3
2	20200421062228_AddProfiles	3.1.3
3	20200430195502_AddReservation	3.1.3
4	20200723115059_Profile_AddSalutation	5.0.0-preview.6.20312.4
5	20200723115153_Profile_AddCountry	5.0.0-preview.6.20312.4
6	20200723115311_Room_AddWithBathroom	5.0.0-preview.6.20312.4
7	20200723115452_Reservation_AddCheckedInCheckedOut	5.0.0-preview.6.20312.4
8	20200723115635_ReservationRemovedCheckedInCheckedOut	5.0.0-preview.6.20312.4
9	20200724050516_MergedMigration	5.0.0-preview.6.20312.4
10	20200826203203_spUpdateProfilesCountry	5.0.0-preview.6.20312.4
11	20200831201342_spGetGuestsForDate	5.0.0-preview.8.20407.4
12	20200903152708_vwRoomsOccupied	5.0.0-preview.8.20407.4
13	20200928045118_AddAddress	5.0.0-preview.8.20407.4
14	20200929205035_AddAddress	5.0.0-preview.8.20407.4
15	20201001080014_AddReservationProfile	5.0.0-preview.8.20407.4
16	20201002081403_ReservationsAddRoomId	5.0.0-preview.8.20407.4
17	20201004194232_ReservationProfileRelation	5.0.0-rc.1.20451.13
18	20201023185035_UpdateGetGuestsForDate	5.0.0-rc.1.20451.13
19	20201024120241_UpdateVwRoomsOccupied	5.0.0-rc.1.20451.13

follows:

If we want to revert the migration, we must execute the command:

```
dotnet ef database update
20201023185035_UpdateGetGuestsForDate
```

Which will bring the database back to row 18, i.e. revert the last migration. The database status will be as follows:

	MigrationId	ProductVersion
1	20200420055438_InitialCreate	3.1.3
2	20200421062228_AddProfiles	3.1.3
3	20200430195502_AddReservation	3.1.3
4	20200723115059_Profile_AddSalutation	5.0.0-preview.6.20312.4
5	20200723115153_Profile_AddCountry	5.0.0-preview.6.20312.4
6	20200723115311_Room_AddWithBathroom	5.0.0-preview.6.20312.4
7	20200723115452_Reservation_AddCheckedInCheckedOut	5.0.0-preview.6.20312.4
8	20200723115635_ReservationRemovedCheckedInCheckedOut	5.0.0-preview.6.20312.4
9	20200724050516_MergedMigration	5.0.0-preview.6.20312.4
10	20200826203203_spUpdateProfilesCountry	5.0.0-preview.6.20312.4
11	20200831201342_spGetGuestsForDate	5.0.0-preview.8.20407.4
12	20200903152708_vwRoomsOccupied	5.0.0-preview.8.20407.4
13	20200928045118_AddAddress	5.0.0-preview.8.20407.4
14	20200929205035_AddAddress	5.0.0-preview.8.20407.4
15	20201001080014_AddReservationProfile	5.0.0-preview.8.20407.4
16	20201002081403_ReservationsAddRoomId	5.0.0-preview.8.20407.4
17	20201004194232_ReservationProfileRelation	5.0.0-rc.1.20451.13
18	20201023185035_UpdateGetGuestsForDate	5.0.0-rc.1.20451.13

As you can see, the last line is missing. The removed migration updated the *vwRoomsOccupied* view and looked like this:

```
public partial class UpdateVwRoomsOccupied : Migration
{
    protected override void Up(MigrationBuilder migrationBuilder)
    {
        var sql = @"
            CREATE OR ALTER VIEW [dbo].[vwRoomsOccupied] AS
                SELECT r.[From], r.[To], ro.Number As RoomNumber,
                    ro.Level, ro.WithBathroom
                FROM ProfileReservation pr
                JOIN Reservations r ON pr.ReservationsId = r.Id
                JOIN Rooms ro ON r.RoomId = ro.Id";

        migrationBuilder.Sql(sql);
    }

    protected override void Down(MigrationBuilder migrationBuilder)
    {
        migrationBuilder.Sql(@"DROP VIEW vwRoomsOccupied");
    }
}
```

When reverting a migration, the *Down* method is performed and the effect of reverting is to remove the *vwRoomsOccupied* view. Deleting a view may not always be a good idea, but it depends on the program you're writing. However, it is worth remembering to fill in the *Down* method accordingly, where it makes sense.

To revert all migrations, use the command:

```
dotnet ef database update 0
```

You can also remove the migration file from the project by executing the command:

```
dotnet ef migrations remove
```

However, to do this, you must first revert your last migration.

You can revert more migrations by executing the command:

```
dotnet ef database update <ostatnia dobra migracja>
```

Merging migrations

Suppose that after repeatedly changing the database schema in the early stages, our project is now stable. We have several migrations that would be more convenient to combine into one that would create a model once, without many small updates. We would then have a clear picture of the changes in our model without too much history.

Let's assume that our migrations are as follows:

▲ 🔒📁 Migrations
    ▷ 🔒 C# 20200420055438_InitialCreate.cs
    ▷ 🔒 C# 20200421062228_AddProfiles.cs
    ▷ 🔒 C# 20200430195502_AddReservation.cs
    ▷ 🔒 C# 20200723115059_Profile_AddSalutation.cs
    ▷ 🔒 C# 20200723115153_Profile_AddCountry.cs
    ▷ 🔒 C# 20200723115311_Room_AddWithBathroom.cs
    ▷ 🔒 C# 20200723115452_Reservation_AddCheckedInCheckedOut.cs
    ▷ 🔒 C# 20200723115635_ReservationRemovedCheckedInCheckedOut.cs
    ▷ 🔒 C# PrimeDbContextModelSnapshot.cs

Merge when we can delete everything

The easiest way to merge all your migrations would be to delete everything! With that, I mean exactly the following process:

▶ Delete the Migrations directory with all migrations
▶ Clear the __EFMigrationHistory table
▶ Delete all tables and other database objects that were added during migration
▶ Create a new migration with all changes

This is a drastic way to merge migrations as we will lose all data. However, it is very simple and may do the job in some cases. Be sure to check what was generated in the merged migration before executing it.

Merge when we want to keep the data

When we want to keep the data, we can't delete all the database objects already created, but we can merge the migration files in our code. Let's see how this can be done.

▶ Remove all migration scripts from the Migrations folder
▶ Add a new migration with the command *dotnet ef migrations add MergedMigration*
▶ Copy the entire file and clean both *Up* and *Down* methods
▶ Upgrade the database and apply blank MergedMigration with *dotnet ef database update* command
▶ Then replace the contents of the MergedMigration file with the previously generated code

As a result, you will only have one migration file. In my example, the __EFMigrationHistory table looks like this.

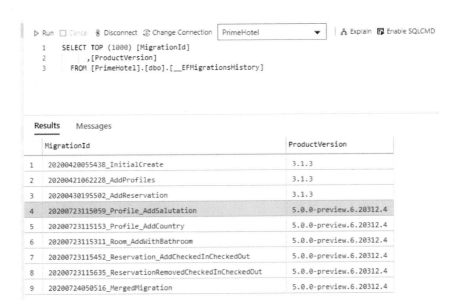

And now I only see one migration in Visual Studio.

▲ 🔒🗔 Migrations
   ▷ + C# 20200724050516_MergedMigration.cs
   ▷ 🔒 C# PrimeDbContextModelSnapshot.cs

Tip! You can also name the merged migration like the first one you've already applied so that you don't have to update the database and add it to the __EFMigrationHistory table.

Merge won't work every time

We can easily combine migrations when they are applied only to the database we control. Additionally, this process will not work in environments that do not have all merged migrations applied. The process is easy, but there are some things you need to pay attention to.

On the other hand, do we have to keep all migrations, even if we know we will never run them again? I don't think so. This is where it would be great to combine the old migrations but keep the most recent ones. This can be achieved in a very similar way.

- ▶ Restore the last N migrations locally, one by one, and copy their contents somewhere
- ▶ Restore the project state to the place matching the migration (git checkout in the right place in the history)
- ▶ Merge all existing migrations
- ▶ Restore the project status to the latest version
- ▶ Add saved recent migrations one by one

In this case, we will keep the latest migrations and create a large initial migration that would fit your design. If there is a case where all migrations must be applied to the database, the database schema will not be corrupted.

Merging migrations in Entity Framework Core 5 is possible, and I can say it's surprisingly easy. It does, however, include an auto-generation process, and you need to check that the merged migration works exactly like all migrations applied individually. Moreover, there is more than one way to combine migrations, and you need to choose the one that is most suitable for you.

Assignments

1. Add a migration engine to your project
2. Add a database update mechanism at project start-up
3. Update the model by adding a field to any entity. Then generate the migration, and:
   a. Upgrade the database using the .NET CLI command
   b. Undo the added migration
   c. Delete the migration file, also using the .NET CLI command
   d. Undo more than one migration
   e. Check the state of the __EFMigrationHistory table on each action

Database First approach

Entity Framework Core does not have a graphical editor, and the Database First approach is very limited. EF 6 allowed to select individual database objects to be attached to the model at each stage of working with the model. EF Core 5 allows for Reverse engineering; however, it is a one-time operation. To do this, we will need a global tool called *dotnet-ef*.

You can install it with the following command:

```
dotnet tool install --global dotnet-ef
```

You can also update the tool after installing it:

```
C:\Windows\system32>dotnet tool install --global dotnet-ef
Tool 'dotnet-ef' is already installed.

C:\Windows\system32>dotnet tool update --global dotnet-ef
Tool 'dotnet-ef' was successfully updated from version '3.1.3' to version '3.1.6'.
```

Using the global ef tool, you can generate models from the database:

```
dotnet ef dbcontext scaffold "Data Source=
localhost;Initial Catalog=PrimeHotel;Integrated
Security=True" Microsoft.EntityFramework-
Core.SqlServer
```

The above command will restore all tables in the database to our model. The scaffolding process requires a connection string to be passed. Here we pass it in the command, but we can also do the job in a more elegant and secure way by just giving it its name and setting it in the appsettings.json file.

In both cases, the effect will be as follows:

Filter files using a regular expression...

➕ PrimeHotel scaffold/Address.cs
➕ PrimeHotel scaffold/PrimeHotelContext.cs
➕ PrimeHotel scaffold/Profile.cs
➕ PrimeHotel scaffold/ProfileReservation.cs
➕ PrimeHotel scaffold/Reservation.cs
➕ PrimeHotel scaffold/Room.cs
➕ PrimeHotel scaffold/VwGuestArrival.cs
➕ PrimeHotel scaffold/VwRoomsOccupied.cs

The effect is satisfactory, but it would be more convenient to have more control over the process.

Adapt the process to your needs

Fortunately, there are more parameters we can use. Let's take a look at some of them:

▶ *--table* can be used to attach specific tables
▶ *--use-database-names* will keep the original database names as far as possible. However, invalid .NET IDs will still be changed
▶ *--context* can be used to give the generated DbContext its own name
▶ *--context-dir* is used to create a DbContext skeleton in the specified directory
▶ *--output-dir* is used to create entity classes in the specified directory
▶ *--force* will overwrite existing DbContext class and entity classes

I modified my command to look like this:

```
dotnet ef dbcontext scaffold "Data
Source=localhost;Initial
Catalog=PrimeHotel;Integrated Security=True"
Microsoft.EntityFrameworkCore.SqlServer --table
Profiles --table Address --context
PrimeHotelDbContext --context-dir Models --
output-dir Models
```

Here are the classes that were generated.

Filter files using a regular expression...

➕ PrimeHotel scaffold/Models/**Address.cs**
➕ PrimeHotel scaffold/Models/**PrimeHotelDbContext.cs**
➕ PrimeHotel scaffold/Models/**Profile.cs**

Note that only the entities for the *Address* and *Profiles* tables were generated, the *DbContext* class is named *PrimeHotelDbContext*, and everything was generated in the *Models* directory. That's it!

Restrictions

▶ Reverse engineering does a tremendous job of scaffolding entity classes so we don't have to write them ourselves. However, there are some limitations to this process:

▶ Not everything about the model is presented in the database schema. For example, inheritance hierarchies, custom types, and split tables will not be recreated

▶ Furthermore, the EF Core documentation claims that there are some column types that will not be included in the model

▶ Nullable types will not be mapped as nullable. For example, string columns that might be null will not be mapped as string ? You have to add this change yourself.

You can read more about it in this Microsoft article:https://docs.microsoft.com/pl-pl/ef/core/managing-schemas/scaffolding?tabs=dotnet-core-cli#limitations

As you can see, the options are quite limited. However, this is expected to change in the future. Microsoft is already working on it, but it's not certain whether or not a real graphics editor will be created.

How it looked in Entity Framework

Entity Framework, the predecessor of Entity Framework Core, is known to have models and database schema description saved in EDMX. One of its components is an entity diagram, which allows you to view, update and modify entities in the model. We can edit our model in a convenient, graphic way.

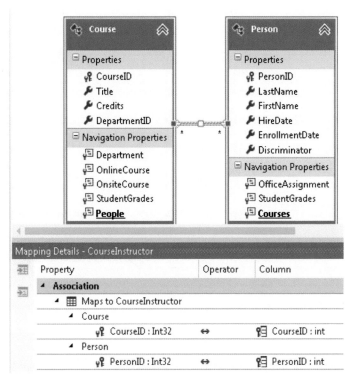

Source: https://docs.microsoft.com/pl-pl/ef/ef6/modeling/designer/relationships

In addition, it also allows you to add an entity from the database, generate a model for it and add a relationship.

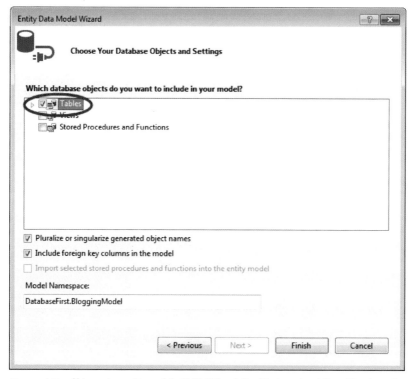

Source: https://docs.microsoft.com/pl-pl/ef/ef6/modeling/designer/workflows/database-first

The graphical editor is much more convenient than writing commands in the console in Entity Framework Core, so it's worth briefly comparing the two approaches.

Entity Framework:

- ▶ It has a convenient graphic editor that clearly shows the relationship between the tables
- ▶ Allows you to update the model by adding a single element
- ▶ Generates convenient code to run stored procedures and functions
- ▶ The model in EF 6 is saved in an EDMX file which is hard to maintain. With a large model, the editor becomes sluggish and difficult to navigate

Entity Framework Core:

- ▶ With the dotnet ef command, dbcontext scaffold allows you to restore the database schema
- ▶ Scaffolding supports only tables (not views), stored procedures, and functions
- ▶ It is not possible to add individual objects to an already generated model. It is only possible to regenerate it
- ▶ Can generate a model with relationships, however a many-to-many relationship is generated with a connecting table, which is not required in EF Core 5 (might change in the future)

Assignments

1. Generate a model for an existing database in several variants
   a. With selected tables
   b. Where the model will be separate from the DbContext class
   c. Where the classes will have a specific namespace
2. Update the model with the *–force* parameter

Creating relationships

Relationships in the context of the database define how two entities are related to each other. Entity Framework Core really shines in the way that it supports relationships. It offers a configuration based on a convention, whereby properly constructing the model, we can generate tables with relationships in the database. In more advanced cases, we can take advantage of the robust capabilities of the Fluent API, which provides more flexibility in saving the configuration.

I must admit that working with relationships in Entity Framework Core 5 is very natural for a developer, and perhaps this is its most important feature.

Database relationships will mean that the two entities are related to each other. They are logically connected. Let's look at the hotel model:

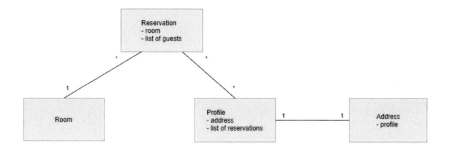

We have a one-room booking with a list of guests. A room can be assigned to multiple bookings. A profile can also be assigned to multiple bookings and is associated with only one address at a time. We have 3 different types of relationships defined here:

▶ one-to-many - room and reservation
▶ many-to-many - reservation and profile
▶ one-to-one - profile and address

These types are well supported by Entity Framework Core, so let's take a look at the model that corresponds to the schema seen above. Here is the *Reservation*:

```
public class Reservation
{
    public int Id { get; set; }

    public int RoomId { get; set; }

    public Room Room { get; set; }

    public List<Profile> Profiles { get; set; }

    public DateTime Created { get; set; }

    public DateTime From { get; set; }

    public DateTime To { get; set; }
}
```

And a *Room*:

```
public class Room
{
    public int Id { get; set; }

    public int Number { get; set; }

    public string Description { get; set; }

    public DateTime LastBooked { get; set; }

    public int Level { get; set; }

    public RoomType RoomType { get; set; }

    public bool WithBathroom { get; set; }

    public int NumberOfPlacesToSleep { get; set; }
}

public enum RoomType
{
    Standard,
    Suite
}
```

And also a *Profile*:

```
public class Profile
{
    public int Id { get; set; }

    public string Ref { get; set; }

    public string Salutation { get; set; }

    public string Forename { get; set; }

    public string Surname { get; set; }

    public string TelNo { get; set; }

    public string Email { get; set; }

    public string Country { get; set; }

    public DateTime? DateOfBirth { get; set; }

    public Address Address { get; set; }

    public List<Reservation> Reservations { get; set; }
}
```

And an *Address*:

```
public class Address
{
    public int Id { get; set; }

    public string Street { get; set; }

    public string HouseNumber { get; set; }

    public string City { get; set; }

    public string PostCode { get; set; }

    public int ProfileId { get; set; }

    public Profile Profile { get; set; }
}
```

And the icing on the cake, *PrimeDbContext*:

```csharp
public class PrimeDbContext : DbContext
{
    public PrimeDbContext(DbContextOptions<PrimeDbContext> options)
        : base(options)
    {
    }

    public virtual DbSet<Room> Rooms { get; set; }

    public virtual DbSet<Profile> Profiles { get; set; }

    public virtual DbSet<Reservation> Reservations { get; set; }

    public virtual DbSet<Address> Address { get; set; }

    // from stored procedures
    public virtual DbSet<GuestArrival> GuestArrivals { get; set; }

    // from views
    public virtual DbSet<RoomOccupied> RoomsOccupied { get; set; }

    protected override void OnModelCreating(ModelBuilder modelBuilder)
    {
    }
}
```

Please note a very important thing: thanks to the convention-based configuration, **no additional configuration is required** in the model classes and the *PrimeDbContext* class.

Configuration in simple

Have you noticed how easy it is to set up relationships in Entity Framework Core 5? If the properties in your model classes are properly named, EF Core will recognize your relationships on its own. The relationship is defined by a navigational property, which is an entity within another entity. Take a look at the reservation. It contains the *Room* entity, i.e. the navigation property, and *RoomId*, which will be treated as a foreign key to defin the relationship.

For relationships to be correctly recognized, remember that:

▶ The primary key in the table should be named Id or <TableName>Id
▶ When adding a navigation property, name it the same as the entity, i.e. if you are adding a *Profiles* entity, name it *Profiles*
▶ If you do not define a foreign key, it will be added automatically by EF Core

More about this is described in the documentation on this page:
https://docs.microsoft.com/pl-pl/ef/core/modeling/relationships?tabs=fluent-api%2Cfluent-api-simple-key%2Csimple-key#fully-defined-relationships

There are 3 ways to configure the model and relationships:

► Convention-based - with appropriately named properties, EF Core decides how entities are related
► Data annotations - useful attributes that can be placed over an entity property
► Fluent API - a full-featured API to configure relationships and entities as you see fit

Here is an example of data annotations to set a custom named foreign key:

```
public class Post
{
    public int PostId { get; set; }
    public string Title { get; set; }
    public string Content { get; set; }

    public int BlogForeignKey { get; set; }

    [ForeignKey("BlogForeignKey")]
    public Blog Blog { get; set; }
}
```

If the name of the foreign key was *BlogId*, it would be automatically configured, but the custom name must be handled manually.

Even with many-to-many relationships, there is no need to define a link table and write additional configuration. This is a new feature since EF Core 5 RC1.

If you do not configure a join table in a many-to-many relationship, it will be generated automatically by EF Core, but not mapped to the

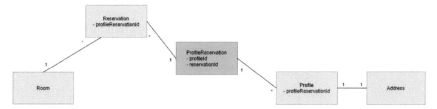

model, so you won't be able to see it. This is a nice convenience as the linking table is an implementation detail rather than a goal itself. In the database, our model will look like this:

Fortunately, in most cases you don't have to manually type a large part of the configuration as this is mostly necessary when dealing with advanced scenarios and custom mappings.

Model First approach

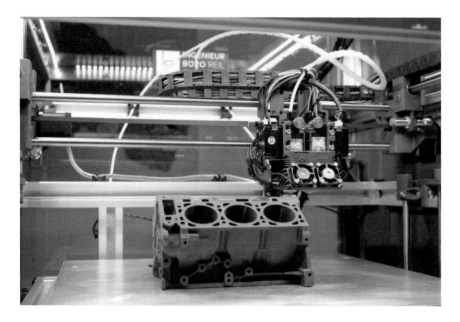

The Model First approach enables you to define the model and relationships and use Entity Framework Core to generate SQL. All you need to do is create the models you want and when you're done, just create a database migration, assuming you already have EF Core migrations.

The mentioned approach also works for updating the model when you need to add a related entity. EF Core migrations will handle it surprisingly well.

Let's say I have a *Profile* entity and we want to add an *Address* entity in a one-to-one relationship. You can take a look at the code for both of these classes above. After adding a new migration using the dotnet CLI, I receive a new migration, already generated, based on my model changes.

```
public partial class AddAddress : Migration
{
    protected override void Up(MigrationBuilder migrationBuilder)
    {
        migrationBuilder.CreateTable(
            name: "Address",
            columns: table => new
            {
                Id = table.Column<int>(type: "int", nullable: false)
                    .Annotation("SqlServer:Identity", "1, 1"),
                Street = table.Column<string>(
                        type: "nvarchar(max)", nullable: true),
                HouseNumber = table.Column<string>(
                        type: "nvarchar(max)", nullable: true),
                City = table.Column<string>(
                        type: "nvarchar(max)", nullable: true),
                PostCode = table.Column<string>(
                        type: "nvarchar(max)", nullable: true),
                ProfileId = table.Column<int>(type: "int", nullable: false)
            },
            constraints: table =>
            {
                table.PrimaryKey("PK_Address", x => x.Id);
                table.ForeignKey(
                    name: "FK_Address_Profiles_ProfileId",
                    column: x => x.ProfileId,
                    principalTable: "Profiles",
                    principalColumn: "Id",
                    onDelete: ReferentialAction.Cascade);
            });

        migrationBuilder.CreateIndex(
            name: "IX_Address_ProfileId",
            table: "Address",
            column: "ProfileId",
            unique: true);
    }

    protected override void Down(MigrationBuilder migrationBuilder)
    {
        migrationBuilder.DropTable(
            name: "Address");
    }
}
```

Easy and fun, but most importantly - it works!

Setting up a relationship in Entity Framework Core 5 is as easy as it gets. Most of the mappings can be done automatically by the framework, simply by naming the property appropriately. If you are struggling with more advanced scenarios, you can use the Fluent API which offers a lot of possibilities with concise notations. In just a few lines you can define, for example, how view is mapped to an entity.

My favourite part, however, is the Model First approach where you build the model you want to work with and generate SQL with EF Core migrations.

Using relationships

In Entity Framework Core, using relationships is very natural. If we want to add an entity that is related to others, all we need to do is assign these objects to ourselves. Using the example above - if we add a profile, we should also assign it an address, because the profile and the address are in a one-to-one relationship. In the code, I add a profile using Swagger in a simple ASP.NET Core application:

And the code looks like this:

```
[HttpPost]
public async Task<IActionResult> Post([FromBody] Profile profile)
{
    var createdProfile = await
primeDbContext.Profiles.AddAsync(profile);
    await primeDbContext.SaveChangesAsync();

    return Ok(createdProfile.Entity);
}
```

In Swagger, the profile with the address is saved as JSON and will be automatically mapped to the *Profile* and *Address* classes. After executing the above code, the profile and address will be added to the database, and both will be linked. We could also download an existing address from the database and assign it to the profile. In this case, the new address will not be added, but will be associated with the added profile.

When we add a new booking, we assume that both the room and guest profiles are already in our database. So, we have a new class called *NewReservation* that we will use to create a new reservation.

```
public class NewReservation
{
    [Required]
    public int RoomId { get; set; }

    [Required]
    public List<int> GuestIds { get; set; }

    [Required]
    public DateTime? From { get; set; }

    [Required]
    public DateTime? To { get; set; }
}
```

Note that here, instead of entering the full room and profiles, we only specify their IDs. The code that will create a new reservation from it looks like this:

```csharp
[HttpPost]
public async Task<IActionResult> Post(
    [FromBody] NewReservation newReservation)
{
    var room = await primeDbContext.Rooms
        .FirstOrDefaultAsync(r => r.Id == newReservation.RoomId);
    var guests = await primeDbContext.Profiles
        .Where(p => newReservation.GuestIds.Contains(p.Id)).ToListAsync();

    if (room == null || guests.Count != newReservation.GuestIds.Count)
    {
        return NotFound();
    }

    var reservation = new Reservation
    {
        Created = DateTime.UtcNow,
        From = newReservation.From.Value,
        To = newReservation.To.Value,
        Room = room,
        Profiles = guests
    };

    var createdReservation = await primeDbContext.Reservations
            .AddAsync(reservation);
    await primeDbContext.SaveChangesAsync();

    return Ok(createdReservation.Entity.Id);
}
```

First, we download the room entity and guest profiles, and then assign it to the newly created reservation. Finally, we save the reservation and all data is saved in the database.

Fetching dependencies in relationships

Please wait while Windows connects to the "Microsoft" network.

In Entity Framework Core, entities that depend on the one downloaded from the database do not need to be loaded immediately. There are 3 methods of fetching the related entities:

- ▶ Eager loading - the dependency is loaded from the database immediately
- ▶ Explicit loading - dependency must be downloaded separately, which can be done at any time
- ▶ Lazy loading - the dependency is downloaded only at the time of its use, without the need to write additional code

Eager loading

We use early loading when we already know that we will need related entities in the program code. It uses the word *Include*.

```
[HttpGet]
public async Task<IEnumerable<Reservation>> Get()
{
    return await primeDbContext.Reservations.Include(r => r.Room)
        .AsNoTracking().ToListAsync();
}
```

In this case, we collect reservations to which we immediately attach the associated room. We can pull many dependencies this way by using *ThenInclude* and even dependencies to dependencies. You can find more examples here: https://docs.microsoft.com/pl-pl/ef/core/querying/related-data/eager.

Explicit loading

We use explicit loading when we want to control when we fetch the data. We then have control over it for each entity separately. In the case of a collection, we use the *Collection* method and *Reference*, if we get a single, dependent entity.

```
[HttpGet("{id}")]
public async Task<IActionResult> GetById(int id)
{
    var reservation = await primeDbContext.Reservations.FindAsync(id);
    if (reservation == null)
    {
        return NotFound();
    }

    await primeDbContext.Entry(reservation).Collection(r => r.Pro-
files).LoadAsync();
    await primeDbContext.Entry(reservation).Reference(r => r.Room).LoadAsync();

    return Ok(reservation);
}
```

We can also filter the retrieved entities immediately, which will be translated into a SQL query in the database.

Lazy loading

We need to work a little more to get delayed loading running. First, we need to install the *Microsoft.EntityFrameworkCore.Proxies NuGet* package, and the properties we want to get in this way must be virtual. There are also more advanced scenarios that are best described in the Microsoft documentation: https://docs.microsoft.com/pl-pl/ef/core/querying/related-data/lazy.

Other operations on the database

Entity Framework Core focuses on working with tables in the database, but it also allows other operations, thanks to which its capabilities are quite extensive. With EF Core, you can conveniently execute a SQL query as well as work with views and stored procedures. In this chapter, I'll discuss how to do this.

Executing a stored procedure

Stored procedures are an integral part of every MS SQL database. They're perfect for wrapping complex SQL code into a reusable database object. How to execute a stored procedure in Entity Framework Core 5? Let's find out.

First of all, we need to add a stored procedure. The best way to do this is to add a database migration with the appropriate SQL code. The generated migration will be empty, and after adding the SQL command that adds the stored procedure, the whole thing will look like this:

```csharp
public partial class spUpdateProfilesCountry : Migration
{
    protected override void Up(MigrationBuilder migrationBuilder)
    {
        var sql = @"
            IF OBJECT_ID('UpdateProfilesCountry', 'P') IS NOT NULL
            DROP PROC UpdateProfilesCountry
            GO

            CREATE PROCEDURE [dbo].[UpdateProfilesCountry]
                @StardId int
            AS
            BEGIN
                SET NOCOUNT ON;
                UPDATE Profiles SET Country = 'Poland'
                WHERE LEFT(TelNo, 2) = '48' AND Id > @StardId
            END";

        migrationBuilder.Sql(sql);
    }

    protected override void Down(MigrationBuilder migrationBuilder)
    {
        migrationBuilder.Sql(@"DROP PROC UpdateProfilesCountry");
    }
}
```

This is a simple SQL code that first checks if a procedure exists and, if so, deletes it. It then creates a new stored procedure with the name *UpdateProfilesCountry* that will update the *Country* column for each profile whose phone number starts with 48.

When the migration is done against the database, it will create the *UpdateProfilesCountry* stored procedure.

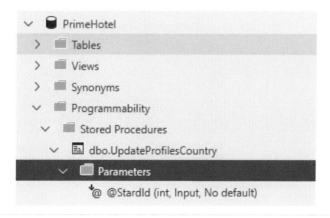

There is no dedicated method for executing a stored procedure in EF Core 5, so in the case where a stored procedure doesn't return data, we can just call it a regular SQL. This can be achieved as follows:

```
await primeDbContext.Database.ExecuteSqlInterpolatedAsync(
    $"UpdateProfilesCountry {minimalProfileId}");
```

When we query the database for all numbers starting with 48, we will see that the country has been updated to Poland. This means that our procedure has been correctly executed.

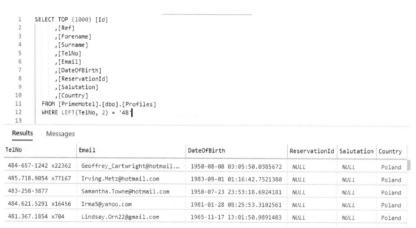

```
1    SELECT TOP (1000) [Id]
2          ,[Ref]
3          ,[Forename]
4          ,[Surname]
5          ,[TelNo]
6          ,[Email]
7          ,[DateOfBirth]
8          ,[ReservationId]
9          ,[Salutation]
10         ,[Country]
11   FROM [PrimeHotel].[dbo].[Profiles]
12   WHERE LEFT(TelNo, 2) = '48'
13
```

Results   Messages

TelNo	Email	DateOfBirth	ReservationId	Salutation	Country
484-657-1242 x22362	Geoffrey_Cartwright@hotmail...	1950-08-08 03:05:50.0385672	NULL	NULL	Poland
485.718.9054 x77167	Irving.Metz@hotmail.com	1983-09-01 01:16:42.7521380	NULL	NULL	Poland
483-258-3877	Samantha.Towne@hotmail.com	1958-07-23 23:53:18.6924181	NULL	NULL	Poland
484.621.5291 x16456	Irma5@yahoo.com	1981-01-28 08:25:53.3102561	NULL	NULL	Poland
481.367.1854 x704	Lindsay.Orn22@gmail.com	1965-11-17 13:01:50.9891483	NULL	NULL	Poland

By the way. Don't worry about seeing real personal information in the example above. These are false data generated with the help of the Bogus library. :)

Getting data with a stored procedure

To see how we can map the data returned by the stored procedure, let's first add one that returns data. We will do it, as in the previous section, with the help of database migration.

```
public partial class UpdateGetGuestsForDate : Migration
{
    protected override void Up(MigrationBuilder migrationBuilder)
    {
        var sql = @"
            IF OBJECT_ID('GetGuestsForDate', 'P') IS NOT NULL
            DROP PROC GetGuestsForDate
            GO

            CREATE PROCEDURE [dbo].[GetGuestsForDate]
                @StartDate varchar(20)
            AS
            BEGIN
                SET NOCOUNT ON;
                SELECT p.Forename, p.Surname, p.TelNo, r.[From], r.[To],
                        ro.Number As RoomNumber
                FROM Profiles p
                JOIN ProfileReservation pr ON pr.ProfilesId = p.Id
                JOIN Reservations r ON pr.ReservationsId = r.Id
                JOIN Rooms ro ON r.RoomId = ro.Id
                WHERE CAST([From] AS date) = CONVERT(date, @StartDate, 105)
            END";

        migrationBuilder.Sql(sql);
    }

    protected override void Down(MigrationBuilder migrationBuilder)
    {
        migrationBuilder.Sql(@"DROP PROC GetGuestsForDate");
    }
}
```

This is the SQL that first checks if the procedure exists and, if so, deletes it. It then creates a new stored procedure called *GetGuestsForDate* that will fetch all arriving guests on that day.

Once the migration is done on the database it will add our stored procedure as we can see here:

When you take a closer look at SQL, you'll notice that we expect to get a guest list with the fields: *Forename, Surname, TelNo, From, To* and *RoomNumber*. To use a stored procedure to query a database and map the results to entities, we need to add the appropriate entity. In my case, I'll add *GuestArrival* which looks like this:

```
[Keyless]
public class GuestArrival
{
    public string Forename { get; set; }

    public string Surname { get; set; }

    public string TelNo { get; set; }

    public DateTime From { get; set; }

    public DateTime To { get; set; }

    public int RoomNumber { get; set; }
}
```

This class contains all the columns I want to map and also has a *[Keyless]* attribute. Keyless entities have most mapping capabilities like regular entities, but are not tracked for changes. It also means that we will not be able to insert, update or delete such an object.

We also need to add the DbSet collection to our *PrimeDbContext*.

```csharp
public class PrimeDbContext : DbContext
{
    public PrimeDbContext(DbContextOptions<PrimeDbContext> options)
        : base(options)
    {
    }

    // from stored procedure
    public virtual DbSet<GuestArrival> GuestArrivals { get; set; }

    protected override void OnModelCreating(ModelBuilder modelBuilder)
    {

    }
}
```

Now we can go ahead and use it. Here's how we can execute this stored procedure in one of the controller methods in ASP.NET Core:

```csharp
[HttpGet("GetGuestsForDate")]
public IActionResult GetGuestsForData([FromQuery] string date)
{
    var guests =
primeDbContext.GuestArrivals.FromSqlInterpolated($"GetGuestsForDate
{date}").ToList();

    return Ok(guests);
}
```

So little code is enough to map objects from a stored procedure. I love Entity Framework Core 5 precisely because of the combination of simplicity and great possibilities!

```csharp
[HttpGet("GetGuestsForDate")]
0 references | Michał Białecki, 31 days ago | 1 author, 2 changes
public IActionResult GetGuestsForData([FromQuery] string date)    date = "04-10-2020"
{
    var guests = primeDbContext.GuestArrivals.FromSqlInterpolated($"GetGuestsForDate {date}").ToList();    guests = Count = 2

    return Ok(guests);    guests = Count = 2
}
                         ◢ ● guests      Count = 2  ◄●
                            ▶ ● [0]            {PrimeHotel.Web.Models.GuestArrival}
[HttpGet("GetRoomsOcc ▶ ● [1]            {PrimeHotel.Web.Models.GuestArrival}
0 references | Michał Białecki, ▶ ● Raw View
public IActionResult GetGuestsArrivalsForView([FromQuery] string date)[...]
```

I'll mention here that I'm using the date parameter in the format *dd-MM-yyyy*, which I pass as a string to my stored procedure. Then I use *CONVERT(date, @StartDate, 105)* in its content, where 105 is the date format I am going to convert. Another possibility is to use the SqlParameter parameter with the *Date* data type, however formatting and passing the date can be cumbersome, so I chose this way.

Watch out! Be very careful when passing parameters to a SQL command. Especially by passing on user-supplied data, you may be exposed to a SQL injection attack. To avoid this, use the *FromSqlInterpolated* or *ExecuteSqlInterpolated* methods. In these methods, we pass the *FormattableString* type, not a regular string. In this way, EF Core is able to check these parameters and make sure they do not contain invalid characters or expressions.

Working with views

A view in the context of databases is a virtual table based on the result set obtained by executing the SQL query. They are typically used as read-only objects that are optimized to deliver data for a given scenario. Entity Framework Core 5 supports views, and in this section, I'll show you how it works.

The first thing we need to do is add a view to the database. The best way to do this is to add a database migration with the appropriate SQL code. Let's start by adding migrations with the EF Core Global Tool command:

```
dotnet ef migrations add vwGuestArrivals
```

This command will generate a migration in which we can put our SQL. Let's see what it might look like:

```
public partial class UpdateVwRoomsOccupied : Migration
{
    protected override void Up(MigrationBuilder migrationBuilder)
    {
        var sql = @"
            CREATE OR ALTER VIEW [dbo].[vwRoomsOccupied] AS
                SELECT r.[From], r.[To], ro.Number As RoomNumber,
                ro.Level, ro.WithBathroom
                FROM ProfileReservation pr
                JOIN Reservations r ON pr.ReservationsId = r.Id
                JOIN Rooms ro ON r.RoomId = ro.Id";

        migrationBuilder.Sql(sql);
    }

    protected override void Down(MigrationBuilder migrationBuilder)
    {
        migrationBuilder.Sql(@"DROP VIEW vwRoomsOccupied");
    }
}
```

This view shows the occupied rooms that we can filter by date. This kind of data can be useful in a hotel, for example when planning cleaning and renovation works.

In Entity Framework Core 5, views can be represented as a regular DbSet collection. In my case, to map all of the view columns, we need to create a *RoomOcupied* model that looks like this:

```
[Keyless]
public class RoomOccupied
{
    public DateTime From { get; set; }

    public DateTime To { get; set; }

    public int RoomNumber { get; set; }

    public int Level { get; set; }

    public bool WithBathroom { get; set; }
}
```

Now we need to add the DbSet collection to *PrimeDbContext* and configure our model to have *RoomsOccupied* execute on a specific view. Let's see how this can be achieved:

```csharp
public class PrimeDbContext : DbContext
{
    public PrimeDbContext(DbContextOptions<PrimeDbContext> options)
        : base(options)
    {
    }

    // from view
    public virtual DbSet<RoomOccupied> RoomsOccupied { get; set; }

    protected override void OnModelCreating(ModelBuilder modelBuilder)
    {
        modelBuilder
            .Entity<RoomOccupied>(eb =>
            {
                eb.HasNoKey();
                eb.ToView("vwRoomsOccupied");
            });
    }
}
```

As you can see, this is a normal DbSet collection that can be filtered as you like. However, there is one little thing that makes this collection unique. Note that we're configuring the *RoomOccupied* entity so that it doesn't have a key. This way, we don't need to have the key in the result, but it also means that it will be a read-only model.

Currently, Entity Framework Core 5 does not support updating entities via view, although it is possible in a SQL Server database. However, you can define a view that has a key. Just remember to remove the *HasNoKey* in the configuration and the *[Keyless]* attribute in the entity.

Let's use the code we just wrote. To do this in the simplest way possible, I added a method to the controller in ASP.NET Core. Here's what it looks like:

```
[HttpGet("GetRoomsOccupied")]
public IActionResult GetGuestArrivalsFromView([FromQuery] string date)
{
    var parsedDate = DateTime.ParseExact(date, "dd-MM-yyyy",
        CultureInfo.InvariantCulture);
    var rooms = primeDbContext.RoomsOccupied.Where(r => r.From <= parsedDate
        && r.To >= parsedDate);

    return Ok(rooms);
}
```

Here I give the date in the format dd-MM-yyyy and ask for all occupied rooms on that day. This is the result.

http://localhost:61099/Profile/GetRoomsOccupied?date=26-07-2020

Server response

Code   Details

200

Response body

```
[
    {
        "from": "2020-07-25T20:52:42.116",
        "to": "2020-07-29T20:52:42.116",
        "roomNumber": 8,
        "level": 0,
        "withBathroom": true
    },
    {
        "from": "2020-07-25T00:00:00",
        "to": "2020-07-30T00:00:00",
        "roomNumber": 7,
        "level": 0,
        "withBathroom": true
    },
    {
        "from": "2020-07-25T00:00:00",
        "to": "2020-07-28T00:00:00",
        "roomNumber": 9,
        "level": 0,
        "withBathroom": true
    }
]
```

I am using *vwRoomsOccupied* and it is executing a SQL query with all filters applied. To see the SQL code being executed, we can run SQL Server Profiler. This Microsoft program will show us all SQL queries along with their execution times and the amount of data transferred.

Note that although I work with the *RoomsOccupied* collection and add C# filtering to it, the SQL command also includes this filtering. This is a fantastic feature of Entity Framework Core as many LINQ commands are supported and mapped to commands in the database.

Executing a SQL command

As you may have already noticed, EF Core doesn't limit the developer to just working with tables. It allows the execution of a SQL command saved as a string. This is the same mechanism as for stored procedures, where we can pass parameters but also map the results to entities.

The execution of the SQL command will look like this:

```
await primeDbContext.Database.ExecuteSqlInterpolatedAsync(
    $"UPDATE Profiles SET Country = 'Poland' WHERE LEFT(TelNo, 2) = '48'");
```

However, mapping the result to entities requires preparing the collection in the DbContext class with the appropriate fields.

```
var guests = primeDbContext.Profiles.FromSqlInterpolated(
    $"SELECT TOP 100 * FROM Profiles ORDER BY Ref").ToList();
```

It's just a few lines of code and it works perfectly! If you want to pass a parameter to a SQL command, you can do it with a variable, or simply paste it into the body of the command with curly brackets.

Watch out! Be very careful when passing parameters to a SQL command. Especially by passing on user-supplied data, you can be exposed to a SQL injection attack. To avoid this, use the *FromSqlInterpolated* or *ExecuteSqlInterpolated* methods. In these methods, we pass the *FormattableString* type, not a regular string. In this way, EF Core is able to check these parameters and make sure they do not contain invalid characters or expressions.

Assignments

1. Create a simple SQL command such as a single line UPDATE and execute it against the database with EF Core.
2. Create a SQL command that will return a result, e.g.:
   a. Simple SELECT from a single table and map the result to an existing entity
   b. A more complicated SELECT that you will map to a new entity
3. Create a view in the database that can be used for example for reporting
   a. Add an entity representing the view result
   b. Map the response to the entities
   c. Add filtering
   d. Use SQL Server Profiler to check what queries are being executed on the database
4. Create a stored procedure and pass parameters to it

Performance

The predecessor of Entity Framework Core is Entity Framework, which still offers a little more than the new guy. However, EF Core was written from scratch, and one of its main goals was speed. So, let's check how EF Core fares compared to its older brother.

This comparison was made by Chad Golden, comparing the performance of adding, updating and deleting 1000 entities. The exact data and code are available on his blog: https://chadgolden.com/blog/comparing-performance-of-ef6-to-ef-core-3

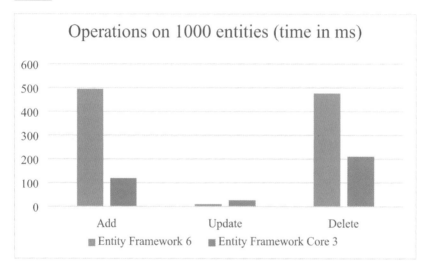

The conclusions are obvious: in almost every test conducted by Chad, Entity Framework Core 3 is faster than Entity Framework 6 – exactly 2.25 to 4.15 times faster! So if performance is important to your application and it operates on large amounts of data, EF Core should be the natural choice.

Is it faster than Dapper?

Dapper is a very popular object-relational mapper and, like EF Core, it facilitates working with the database. It's called the king of Micro ORM because it's very fast and does some of the work for us. If we compare EF Core and Dapper, we immediately notice that the capabilities of EF Core are much greater. Microsoft technology allows you to track objects, migrate the database schema, and interact with the database without writing SQL queries. Dapper, on the other hand, maps the objects returned by the database, but all SQL commands have to be written yourself. This certainly allows more freedom in operating the database, but there is a greater risk of making a mistake when writing a SQL query. Similarly to updating the database schema, EF Core can create changes and generate a migration by itself, and in Dapper you have to manually edit the SQL code.

There is no doubt, however, that Dapper has its supporters, mainly due to its performance. On the blog exceptionnotfound.net we can find a comparison between Entity Framework Core 3 and Dapper version 2.

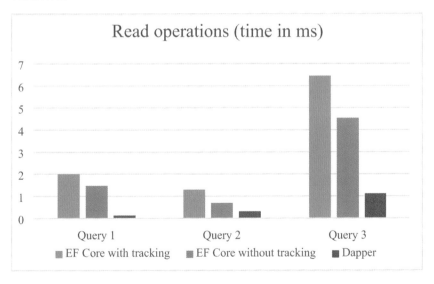

As you can see, we compare 3 database reads here, where Entity Framework Core with object tracking in one case, non-tracking in the other and Dapper's third. Tracking changes to entities in EF Core can be turned off with the *AsNoTracking()* option, which makes reading operations significantly faster. More information on this test can be found here: https://exceptionnotfound.net/dapper-vs-entity-framework-core-query-performance-benchmarking-2019/

All in all - Dapper is much faster to read from the database and will certainly be comparatively fast when writing. However, it requires writing SQL queries, which can expose the developer to errors. I have personally used Dapper on several projects, and basically only one has been dictated by performance. For the simple logic of saving and retrieving data from the database, I would use Entity Framework Core because of its simplicity and convenience in introducing changes.

Assignments

1. In the PrimeHotel project you can generate a large number of guest profiles yourself. This is done using the *GenerateAndInsert* method in the *ProfileController* controller. With the completed table, you can check for yourself how fast individual CRUD operations take and how filtering affects the time of their execution.

2. In the PrimeHotel project you will find the *ProfileWithDapperController* and *ProfilesRepository* classes. It is a repository and controller where you will find CRUD operations on the *Profiles* table written with Dapper.
   a. Compare the differences in the controller
   b. Take a look at *ProfilesRepository*, note as parameters we can pass entire objects
   c. Check how we add related objects in relationships such as *Address* in EF Core and how this can be achieved with Dapper
   d. Try adding filtering of profiles by name so that filtering is done on the database side
   e. If multiple filtering options need to be added, will the code still be readable?

Writing in-memory unit tests

Tests are an integral part of software development. These are separate programs that allow you to check if a piece of a program written by us does exactly what it should. Unit tests are small pieces of code that test individual program elements.

Microsoft recommends that when writing tests that use EF Core, you should use a real database whenever possible. In fact, it is best to use the database in exactly the same configuration and on the same server on which our application will run. This approach may not make sense when it comes to cost, as Microsoft also admits. Performance tests should certainly check our solutions in an environment as close to production as possible. However, when writing unit tests, it's enough to keep the database in memory. Entity Framework Core allows you to run on a virtual database created only in memory. We can also use the SQLite database because it works fast and does not need a server. It also has a mode in which it can run in memory. In this chapter, we won't go into detail about using SQLite for testing, but I can assure you that it doesn't take much effort.

Entity Framework Core 5 is very easy to configure to run in memory and in a test project. Just install the NuGet package called *Microsoft.EntityFrameworkCore.InMemory*, but also a few more might come in handy. Let's check out the full list:

- ▶ Microsoft.EntityFrameworkCore.InMemory – to run EF Core 5 in memory
- ▶ NUnit – a framework to write and run unit tests
- ▶ NUnit3TestAdapter – an adapter to run NUnit tests in Visual Studio
- ▶ FluentAssertions – easy library to write nice and readable assertions

For testing, I will use the *ReservationController* class. Here is its full content:

```csharp
[ApiController]
[Route("[controller]")]
public class ReservationsController : ControllerBase
{
    private readonly PrimeDbContext primeDbContext;

    public ReservationsController(PrimeDbContext _primeDbContext)
    {
        primeDbContext = _primeDbContext;
    }

    [HttpGet]
    public async Task<IEnumerable<Reservation>> Get()
    {
        return await primeDbContext. Reservations
                .Include(r => r.Room).AsNoTracking().ToListAsync();
    }

    [HttpGet("{id}")]
    public async Task<IActionResult> GetById(int id)
    {
        var reservation = await primeDbContext.Reservations.FindAsync(id);
        if (reservation == null)
        {
            return NotFound();
        }

        await primeDbContext.Entry(reservation)
                .Collection(r => r.Profiles).LoadAsync();
        await primeDbContext.Entry(reservation)
                .Reference(r => r.Room).LoadAsync();

        return Ok(reservation);
    }

    [HttpPost]
    public async Task<IActionResult> Post(
                [FromBody] NewReservation newReservation)
    {
        var room = await primeDbContext.Rooms
            .FirstOrDefaultAsync(r => r.Id == newReservation.RoomId);
        var guests = await primeDbContext.Profiles
            .Where(p => newReservation.GuestIds.Contains(p.Id))
            .ToListAsync();

        if (room == null || guests.Count != newReservation.GuestIds.Count)
        {
            return NotFound();
        }

        var reservation = new Reservation
        {
            Created = DateTime.UtcNow,
            From = newReservation.From.Value,
            To = newReservation.To.Value,
            Room = room,
            Profiles = guests
        };
```

```
        var createdReservation = await primeDbContext.Reservations
            .AddAsync(reservation);
        await primeDbContext.SaveChangesAsync();

        return Ok(createdReservation.Entity.Id);
    }
}
```

I named the test class *ReservationControllerTests*, which is the name
of the class and the Tests ending at the end. In these tests, I will focus
on checking how to replace data in Entity Framework Core, and not to
test all possible cases.

The basis here is the appropriate preparation of *PrimeDbContext* for testing. The very base of the class with tests looks like this:

```
public class ReservationsControllerTests
{
    private DbContextOptions<PrimeDbContext> dbContextOptions = new
DbContextOptionsBuilder<PrimeDbContext>()
        .UseInMemoryDatabase(databaseName: "PrimeDb")
        .Options;
    private ReservationsController controller;

    [OneTimeSetUp]
    public void Setup()
    {
        SeedDb();

        controller = new ReservationsController(
            new PrimeDbContext(dbContextOptions));
    }

    private void SeedDb()
    {
        using var context = new PrimeDbContext(dbContextOptions);
        var rooms = new List<Room>
        {
            new Room { Id = 1, Description = "Room nr 1", Number = 1,
                    Level = 1, RoomType = RoomType.Standard },
            new Room { Id = 2, Description = "Room nr 2", Number = 2,
                    Level = 1, RoomType = RoomType.Standard },
            new Room { Id = 3, Description = "Room nr 3", Number = 3,
                    Level = 2, RoomType = RoomType.Suite }
        };
```

```
var profiles = new List<Profile>
{
    new Profile { Id = 1, Ref = "Profile 1",
            Forename = "Michał", Surname = "Białecki" },
    new Profile { Id = 2, Ref = "Profile 2",
            Forename = "John", Surname = "Show" },
    new Profile { Id = 3, Ref = "Profile 3",
            Forename = "Daenerys", Surname = "Targaryen" }
};

context.AddRange(rooms);
context.AddRange(profiles);

context.AddRange(new List<Reservation>
{
    new Reservation
    {
        Id = 1,
        Room = rooms[0],
        Profiles = new List<Profile>{ profiles[0] },
        From = DateTime.Today,
        To = DateTime.Today.AddDays(2)
    },
    new Reservation
    {
        Id = 2,
        Room = rooms[2],
        Profiles = new List<Profile>{ profiles[1], profiles[2] },
        From = DateTime.Today.AddDays(1),
        To = DateTime.Today.AddDays(3)
    }
});

context.SaveChanges();
    }
}
```

The first thing that immediately catches our attention is the *SeedDb* method, which is used to add test data to the EF Core context. For these tests, the data will be entered only once, at the very beginning thanks to the *[OneTimeSetUp]* attribute. The state of the database will be preserved as long as the process that performs these tests is running. However, the more important part is at the top, which is creating a dbContextOptions. Note that this is where we use the UseInMemoryDatabase option, and then create the *PrimeDbContext* class using this object. When creating, we give the name of the database and always use the same one. Another very important line is:

```
using var context = new PrimeDbContext(dbContextOptions);
```

At first, we use the using keyword because we don't want Garbage Collector to remove the context variable from memory while the test is running.

Since we already have a configured database and data, it's time to test:

```
[Test]
public async Task Get_FetchesReservationsWithoutRoomsAndGuests()
{
    using var context = new PrimeDbContext(dbContextOptions);
    var reservations = (await controller.Get()).ToList();

    reservations.Count.Should().Be(2);
    reservations.All(r => r.Room == null).Should().BeTrue();
    reservations.All(r => r.Profiles == null).Should().BeTrue();
}
```

In the first test, we get all reservations and check if their dependencies are loaded. In this case, it won't, because the *Get* method in the controller doesn't force dependencies to be loaded. Let's check another method.

```
[Test]
public async Task
GetById_WhenIdIsProvided_FetchesReservationWithRoomsAndGuests()
{
    using var context = new PrimeDbContext(dbContextOptions);
    var result = await controller.GetById(2);
    var okResult = result.As<OkObjectResult>();
    var reservation = okResult.Value.As<Reservation>();

    reservation.Should().NotBeNull();
    reservation.Profiles.Should().NotBeNull();
    reservation.Room.Should().NotBeNull();
}
```

In the second test, we take a single booking and here we check that both the room and the profiles are loaded. This is because in the *GetById* method, we use the *Collection* and *Reference* methods to load these dependencies. Now let's test the Post method.

The last test checks if the added reservation was added correctly. We check whether the room and the guest's profile have been properly assigned to the new reservation.

Unit testing in Entity Framework Core is really simple and understandable. Only a few lines of configuration allow us to use the dbContext class to prepare the desired database state. We do not have to replace individual collections in *PrimeDbContext* separately, as was the case with the Entity Framework tests. In this respect, Entity Framework Core is refined, and the unit testing using it does not differ significantly from any other unit tests. Working with them is easy and fun, which is exactly as it should be!

More?

If you don't have enough information yet, I will gladly suggest more reading. On the Internet and on the official Microsoft website you will find a lot of interesting information. I have collected some issues here that may interest you.

Ef Core is not only for MS SQL Server

In fact, EF Core supports many database systems. The most interesting are: SQ Lite, Azure Cosmos DB, IBM Db2, or Oracle DB. Certainly not all options are available for all of these providers, but this does not disqualify any. For more details, see: https://docs.microsoft.com/pl-pl/ef/core/providers/?tabs=dotnet-core-cli.

Entity Framework 6 compared to EF Core

What exactly does Entity Framework 6 support and what else is missing from Entity Framework Core 5? As EF Core developed, developers filled more and more gaps between these frameworks. You can find an exact comparison here: https://docs.microsoft.com/pl-pl/ef/efcore-and-ef6/.

How EF Core is handling LINQ queries

LINQ's capabilities are fantastic, Entity Framework Core can turn methods such as *Where* and *GroupBy* directly into SQL queries. But will it handle more complex queries just as well? Find out here: https://docs.microsoft.com/pl-pl/ef/core/querying/complex-query-operators

Combining OData and EF Core

OData is a convention for building REST APIs to easily filter resources using parameters in a URL. It sounds quite enigmatic, but in practice it is very simple and flexible. In addition, if we combine OData with EF Core and the IQuerable interface, then in a few lines we can filter and group our database in the form of a REST API. You can find the post and application code here:
https://www.michalbialecki.com/2020/03/19/odata-as-a-flexible-data-feed-for-react-search/

And if all this is still not enough, be sure to subscribe to my newsletter to receive more interesting information from me:
https://www.michalbialecki.com/newsletter/

The end

Thank you for taking the time to read this book. I gathered the knowledge about Entity Framework Core 5 from the most practical side and explored the parts that I personally found interesting and useful at work. EF Core's capabilities are really big, and the framework itself is mature and stable. Nevertheless, this book is by no means exhaustive, and I encourage you to continue your studies in this direction. Stay tuned to my blog as there will be more EF Core material coming.

I am curious about your thoughts on this book. Did you learn anything new thanks to it? Or maybe something surprised you? Perhaps there is something worth describing more broadly? I encourage you to write to blog@michalbialecki.com with all your comments.

Thanks again and hope to see you in person someday!

Printed in Great Britain
by Amazon